472731

P9-AOO-301

FRIENDS
OF THE MISSISSIPPI LIBRARY SYSTEM

Thank you for your
SUPPORT.

MAY 08 2013

MAY 08 2013

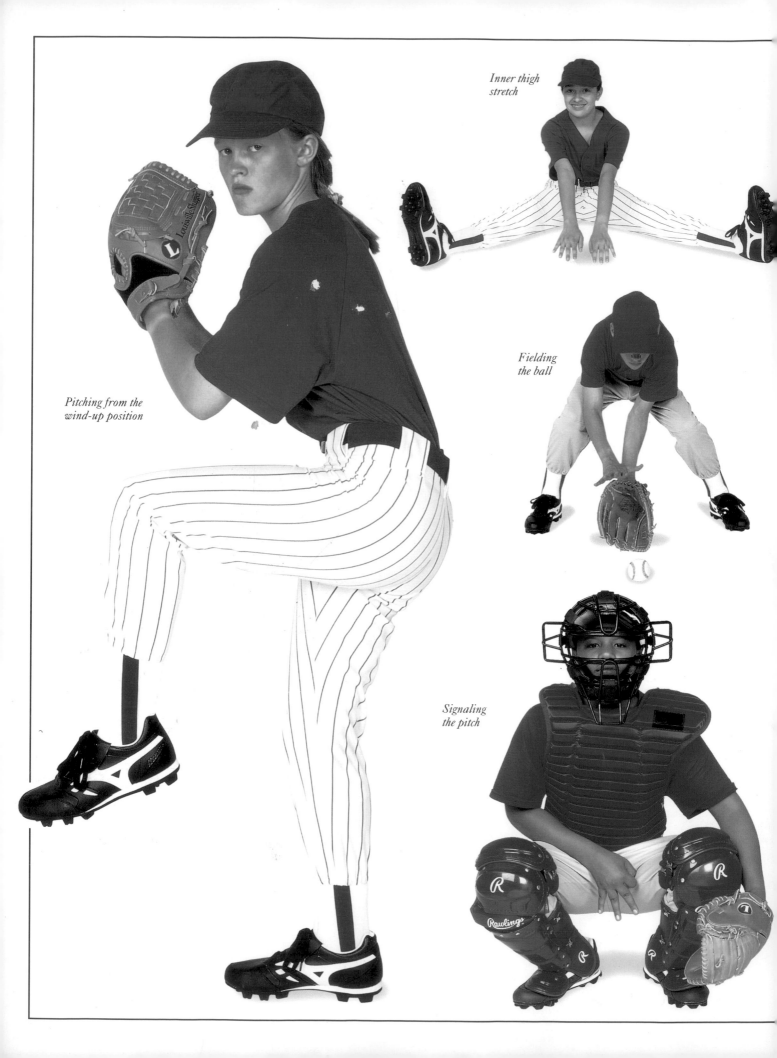

*Inner thigh
stretch*

*Fielding
the ball*

*Pitching from the
wind-up position*

*Signaling
the pitch*

THE YOUNG BASEBALL PLAYER

Written by Ian Smyth
With a foreword by Eduardo Perez

Aluminum baseball bat

Proper batting stance

Fielding an outfield ground ball

Relaxed fielding position

Swinging in the strike zone

Tag plays

Blocking the ball

Stoddart

A DK PUBLISHING BOOK

Project editor Fiona Robertson **Project art editor** Rebecca Johns

US Editor Kristin Ward **DTP designer** Nicky Studdart

Photography Andy Crawford

Senior Managing Editor Gill Denton

Senior Managing Art Editor Julia Harris

Picture Research Sam Ruston

Production Charlotte Traill

The Young Baseball Players
Adam Castle, Jenny Paradine, Durvell Smith
Shyvonne Smith, Rebecca Torres

First published in Canada in 1998 by
Stoddart Publishing Co. Limited
34 Lesmill Road, Toronto, Canada M3B 2T6

First published in Great Britain in 1998 by
Dorling Kindersley Limited
9 Henrietta Street, London WC2E 8PS

Copyright © 1998 Dorling Kindersley Limited

All rights reserved under International and Pan-American Copyright Conventions. No part of this publication
may be reproduced, stored in a retrieval system, or transmitted in any form or by any means, electronic,
mechanical, photocopying, recording, or otherwise, without the prior written permission of the copyright owner.
Published in Great Britain by Dorling Kindersley Limited.

Canadian Cataloguing in Publication Data
Smyth, Ian, 1962–
The young baseball player

(The young enthusiast series)
Includes index
ISBN 0-7737-3076-1
1. Baseball – Juvenile literature. I. Title. II. Series.
GV867.5.S638 1998 j796.357 C97–932306–1

Color reproduction by Colourscan, Singapore
Printed and bound in Italy by L.E.G.O.

Contents

8
To all young baseball players

10
What you will need

12
Warming up

14
The playing field

16
Basic skills – Throwing

18
Basic skills – Fielding

20
Defensive skills – First
and third bases

22
Defensive skills – Second base

24
Defensive skills – Shortstop

26
Defensive skills – Pitching
and grips

28
Defensive skills – Catching

30
The outfield

32
Offensive skills – Hitting
and bunting

34
Offensive skills – Baserunning

36
Taking it further and Glossary

37
Index and Acknowledgments

To all young baseball players

"I ALWAYS KNEW I had a love for the game of baseball – I think it's in my blood. But it wasn't until college at Florida State that I realized I wanted to make a career out of it. Of course, it didn't happen overnight. In fact, I had many lessons to learn and hills to climb. But with discipline and self-confidence, I learned how to overcome all the obstacles. I believe along any journey to success, you must learn from all your mistakes and failures, and allow those lessons to make you stronger. Today, I am proud to be a Major League baseball player with the Cincinnati Reds and still find a challenge in every game I play. I think the most important key to moving forward is to never lose sight of why I started playing in the first place – my ultimate love for the game!"

"I am proud to wear a Cincinnati Reds uniform. It symbolizes both a great ball club, and a special connection with my dad, who sported a Reds uniform during his baseball career!"

"As a former ballplayer himself, my dad, Tony, can offer me valuable hints and tips on improving my game. I know he enjoys watching the whole team play, but he always keeps his eye on number 39, the number I've worn since I joined the Reds."

"You have to keep in good shape so that you can break out of the box with speed and power as soon as you've hit the ball. During pre-season spring training, ballplayers do weight-lifting, running and sliding drills, and batting and throwing exercises, and take daily batting practice during the season."

"You always have to keep your head in the game. It's important to pay attention and concentrate, even when it's quiet, because the next moment a ball might be zooming in your direction."

"A split second can make the difference between being safe or out on the bases, so you've always got to hustle. Playing six or seven games a week during the season helps players get used to handling tough situations with speed and skill."

History of baseball

Elysian Fields, 1846
The first game to be played under the Cartwright Rules was held in 1846 at the Elysian Fields in New Jersey. The Knickerbockers beat the New York Nines by 23–1 and Alexander Cartwright, the writer of the rules, umpired the game.

THE EXACT ORIGINS of baseball are shrouded in mystery and doubt, but it is thought that it developed from the English game of rounders, which was brought to America in the early 1600s by the first English settlers. Different forms of the game were played in different parts of America, but all involved hitting a pitched ball with a stick or bat and trying to score runs. In 1846, Alexander Cartwright wrote a set of rules that form the basis of modern baseball. Today, baseball is the top sport in America and is played in over 100 countries around the world.

YOUNG LADY BASEBALLISTS.
THE VERY NOVEL AND ALREADY SUCCESSFUL IDEA OF MANAGER W. S. FRANKLIN WITH THE BELLES OF THE BALL AND BAT.

Women's baseball
Women have never played in any Major League baseball games, but there have been women's professional baseball teams, most notably during the war. This league was made famous by the movie "A League of Their Own", which told the story of the All American Girls' Professional Baseball League from 1943–54.

The first club
The first professional baseball club, the Cincinnati Red Stockings, was formed in 1869. Their manager was Harry Wright of Sheffield, England. The Red Stockings toured the US, playing against local teams.

Adrian "Cap" Anson
Anson was perhaps the most influential player in the 19th century. He played in the first professional league, the National Association, and was the first man to reach 3,000 hits.

An international interest
Amateur baseball is played throughout the world, with slight variations. In this picture of a game played in Montreal, Canada, in the 1950s, for example, the umpire is wearing his chest protector outside his shirt.

A major breakthrough
One of the most important events in modern baseball occurred in 1947. Up until that date, baseball had been a segregated sport, with separate leagues for black players. However, during that year, Jackie Robinson opened the season at second base for the Brooklyn Dodgers. Robinson was the first black player to play in the major leagues.

Babe Ruth
Babe Ruth was one of the most famous players in the history of baseball, He joined the New York Yankees in 1920. During his 22-year career, the powerful left-hander hit 714 home runs – a record until 1974!

What you will need

ALL YOU REALLY NEED to play baseball is a bat, a ball, and a glove. However, to get the most enjoyment from the game, you should also have all the necessary safety equipment. Baseball is a hard-ball game, and protective equipment for the catcher, batter, and base runners is mandatory. When playing in a league, each team has its own colors and logo and players wear identical uniforms, making them look neat and professional.

The baseball cap is part of the culture and tradition of baseball.

A baseball shirt should look sharp and be comfortable

Baseball uniform
Players in baseball teams often wear a full baseball uniform. This consists of a cap, which is usually embroidered with the team logo, a baseball shirt with the team name and the player's number on it, and an undershirt. The uniform also includes baseball pants and a pair of stirrups, that are worn over athletic socks.

Stirrups
Stirrups are peculiar to baseball. They are pull-over socks that are worn over athletic socks, and are colored to match team uniforms.

Undershirt
Players may wear an undershirt under their team shirt. The undershirt is long-sleeved and is made of cotton so that it absorbs perspiration.

Cup

Athletic supporter

It is important to get a baseball glove or mitt that is comfortable for you.

The cup
It is vital for boys to wear a protective cup when playing. This should be worn with an athletic supporter or a jock strap.

Cleats
Cleats are similar to soccer shoes, except they have cleats or bars on the sole instead of studs. They help a player grip the ground when they play.

Baseball pants come about halfway down your calf.

A professional kit
In the major leagues, each player's uniform is custom-made to fit their build and to match the rest of the team's uniforms. Some players, like Eduardo Perez, prefer to wear their baseball pants long, hitting at the ankle, while other players prefer knee-length pants.

A sports bag should be big enough for all your equipment, including your bat.

Colored stirrups can denote a team name, such as the Boston Red Sox.

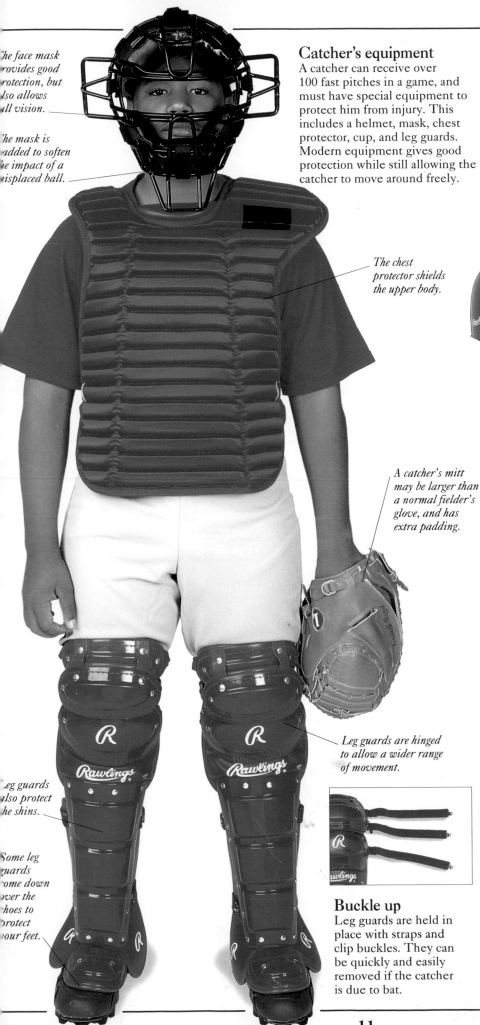

The face mask provides good protection, but also allows full vision.

The mask is padded to soften the impact of a misplaced ball.

Catcher's equipment

A catcher can receive over 100 fast pitches in a game, and must have special equipment to protect him from injury. This includes a helmet, mask, chest protector, cup, and leg guards. Modern equipment gives good protection while still allowing the catcher to move around freely.

The chest protector shields the upper body.

A catcher's mitt may be larger than a normal fielder's glove, and has extra padding.

Leg guards are hinged to allow a wider range of movement.

Leg guards also protect the shins.

Some leg guards come down over the shoes to protect your feet.

Buckle up

Leg guards are held in place with straps and clip buckles. They can be quickly and easily removed if the catcher is due to bat.

Basic equipment

There are several essential items that you will need to play baseball successfully and safely.

Catcher's helmet

This is mandatory in baseball, and will protect you from swinging bats and balls.

Batting helmet

The batter and any base runners must wear a helmet. The helmet consists of a plastic shell with foam inserts. It protects the head and face from a thrown or batted ball.

Catcher's mitt

The catcher receives the ball over a hundred times during a game. This large mitt has extra padding to protect his hand.

Fielder's glove

Gloves are made of leather and come in a variety of sizes. Pitchers and outfielders use large gloves; infielders use smaller gloves.

Batting glove

Gloves are worn to get a really firm grip on the bat. Players can wear two, or just one on their bottom hand.

Bats

Bats come in various lengths and weights and can be made from either aluminum or wood. When choosing a bat, remember that a lighter bat is easier to swing.

Baseball

The ball is made of a cork core wrapped with string and covered in leather. It weighs 5 oz (140 g).

Warming up

IT IS VITAL that you warm up before every game, to help you prepare both physically and mentally for the task ahead. Before you start any stretching routine, it is important to loosen up the muscles. Stretching cold muscles can lead to injury, so you should always run at a steady pace for at least five minutes beforehand. It is important to stretch in a slow, systematic way from head to toe, avoiding bouncing or any sharp movements.

Neck stretch

When you stretch your neck, it is vital that you do all the stretches very slowly and deliberately. Avoid any jerky or sudden movements and never roll your neck. Make sure you stretch it in all directions.

1 Slowly bring the chin down onto the chest. This stretches the back of the neck.

2 Straighten up your head and look straight ahead.

3 Carefully tilt your head back and look up

Calf stretch

To stretch the calf muscle, make sure your hips are facing forward and both feet are pointing directly ahead. Slowly lunge forward, placing your weight over the front knee. The back heel must stay in contact with the ground to ensure that the calf is fully stretched.

Make sure your back heel stays in contact with the ground.

The front foot faces forward.

Arm stretch

Throwing is a crucial part of baseball and you should always stretch your arms before you start to play. Bring one arm across your body and take the other arm up to support it. Pull on the extended arm to stretch the upper arm and shoulder.

Feel the stretch in the upper arm and shoulder.

This arm interlocks and helps the stretch.

Gently push the elbow down.

Waist stretch

You can rest your hands lightly on your hips.

Make sure your shoulders are relaxed.

Your feet should face forward throughout the stretch.

Feel the stretch in your waist.

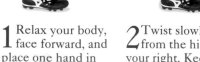 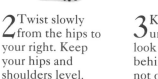

1 Relax your body, face forward, and place one hand in front and one hand behind.

2 Twist slowly from the hips to your right. Keep your hips and shoulders level.

3 Keep twisting until you can look directly behind you. Do not overstretch.

Triceps stretch

The triceps muscle is at the back of the arm. To stretch it, place your arm above your head and gently push down the elbow. This also stretches the shoulder area.

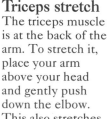

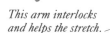

Hold this stretch for 15–20 seconds and then repeat on the other side.

This works the left side of the neck.

Tilt your head toward your shoulder. Do not lift your shoulder up to your head.

2 Move your head back to its normal position, and look straight ahead.

3 Tilt your head slowly toward the other shoulder, stretching the right side of your neck.

Inner thigh stretch

Sit on the floor with your legs apart. Keep the upper body square, place your hands together and stretch them out in front of you. You will feel this stretch in your inner thighs and hamstrings.

Do not bounce. This stretch must be performed slowly.

Flex the feet so that the toes are pointing upward.

Side stretch

To stretch the muscles of the trunk and side, keep the hips square and place one hand on your hip and the other above your head. Slowly stretch down to the side, making sure that you reach downward, not forward.

One arm is above your head.

The hips must stay square.

Place one hand on your hip.

You can increase the stretch by pushing your foot down into your hand.

Thigh stretch

If you find it difficult to balance for this stretch, use a partner or lean against a wall or fence.

1 Pull the heel up to your bottom. Try to stay balanced and hold for 15–20 seconds.

2 To make the stretch harder, pull your bent leg out to the side slightly. Be careful not to lock the knee of your supporting leg.

{ **Easing up**
Try to increase each stretch slightly when you feel the tension in your muscles start to ease. Remember to do all the stretches on the other side, too!

Bend your knees slightly.

Increase this stretch by pulling on the bent leg.

Lower back stretch

Sit on the ground and place one leg over the other. With one arm over the bent leg, stretch the upper body in the opposite direction. You should feel this stretch in the lower back, and also in the back of your thighs and your bottom.

The playing field

A BASEBALL FIELD is made up of the infield, the outfield, and foul territory. Two foul lines run from home plate through first and third bases to create a 90° arc. The infield is the inner part of the arc. A base is placed on each corner of the infield, 90 ft (28 m) apart, to form the diamond. The outfield is the outer part of the baseball field. It is formed by the two foul lines extending to an outfield fence, which should be at least 250 ft (76 m) from home plate. The area inside the foul lines is known as fair territory; the area outside is foul territory.

Different diamonds
In youth league games, the distance between the bases varies from 50–90 ft (15–28 m), depending on the ages and affiliation of the team.

A large scoreboard keeps fans informed of the score in the game they are watching, and in games being played elsewhere.

Camden Yards, Baltimore
One of the finest stadiums in Major League baseball is Camden Yards, the home field of the Baltimore Orioles. Like many major league ballparks, the stadium has been built to combine modern-day luxuries with the timeless attributes of a baseball game. Refreshments are brought to fans as they watch the game, every seat has a great view of the action, and key plays are reshown on the huge video screens.

The game

Winning a game
The object of the game is to score more runs than the opposition. To score a run, the batter/runner must touch each base in turn, and return to home base.

Officials
The rules of the game are enforced by a crew of umpires. In the major leagues there are four umpires per game. In youth baseball, there are usually two – one home plate umpire and one base umpire.

Game duration
An inning is completed when each team has had a turn at batting and at fielding. A standard baseball game lasts for nine innings. Each team has three outs per inning. The number of innings may be reduced in youth baseball.

Extra innings
A baseball game cannot end in a tie. One team has to win and extra innings must be played to ensure a result.

Offense and defense
The team that is batting is said to be playing offense, and the fielding team is the defense team.

Batting order
Before the game begins, the manager of each team decides on the batting order. This is written down and handed to the umpire. It cannot be changed during the game.

Substitutes
Substitutes can be used in a baseball game. However, once a player has been taken out of a game, he cannot return.

Field positions

Position	Abbreviation	Number
Pitcher	p	1
Catcher	c	2
First base	1b	3
Second base	2b	4
Third base	3b	5
Shortstop	ss	6
Left field	lf	7
Center field	cf	8
Right field	rf	9

Base
There are three bases, one in each corner of the diamond. Each base is filled with foam and covered with white canvas. It measures 15 x 15 in (38 x 38 cm) and is secured to the ground. When running the bases (see page 34), you must touch the base, or you may be called out.

Home plate
Home plate is the central focus of the baseball field. It is a five-sided piece of rubber, 17 in (42 cm) across. There is a batter's box on either side of home plate and the catcher's box is behind it.

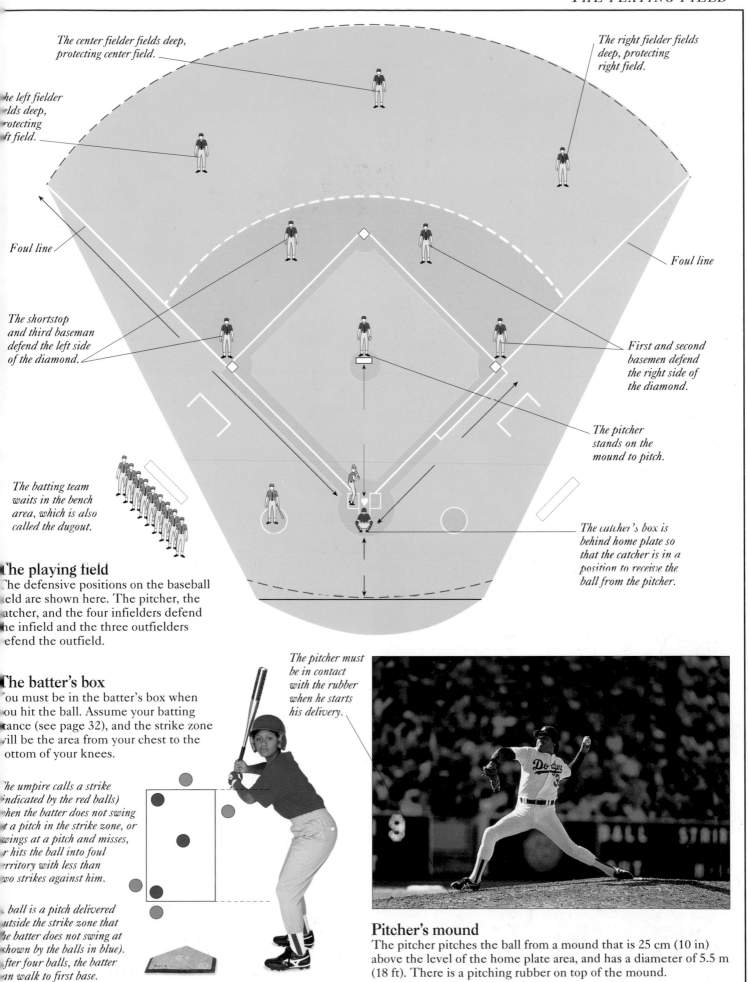

The center fielder fields deep, protecting center field.

The right fielder fields deep, protecting right field.

The left fielder fields deep, protecting left field.

Foul line

Foul line

The shortstop and third baseman defend the left side of the diamond.

First and second basemen defend the right side of the diamond.

The pitcher stands on the mound to pitch.

The batting team waits in the bench area, which is also called the dugout.

The catcher's box is behind home plate so that the catcher is in a position to receive the ball from the pitcher.

The playing field
The defensive positions on the baseball field are shown here. The pitcher, the catcher, and the four infielders defend the infield and the three outfielders defend the outfield.

The batter's box
You must be in the batter's box when you hit the ball. Assume your batting stance (see page 32), and the strike zone will be the area from your chest to the bottom of your knees.

The umpire calls a strike (indicated by the red balls) when the batter does not swing at a pitch in the strike zone, or swings at a pitch and misses, or hits the ball into foul territory with less than two strikes against him.

A ball is a pitch delivered outside the strike zone that the batter does not swing at (shown by the balls in blue). After four balls, the batter can walk to first base.

The pitcher must be in contact with the rubber when he starts his delivery.

Pitcher's mound
The pitcher pitches the ball from a mound that is 25 cm (10 in) above the level of the home plate area, and has a diameter of 5.5 m (18 ft). There is a pitching rubber on top of the mound.

Throwing

T HROWING IS THE primary skill needed to play baseball, and is the key to any defensive position in the game. Correct throwing mechanics also form the basis of pitching. Learning to throw correctly takes time and practice. The sequences shown here highlight two of the most basic techniques that you need to master.

1 To start a play, you must field the ball quickly and cleanly. Make sure your body is directly in front of the ball as you bend to retrieve it.

Bring your arms into your body as you field the ball.

Bend your upper body over the ball.

Sidearm throw to base

This throw is occasionally used by the second baseman or shortstop to cover relatively short distances, when a quick return is needed. The shortstop also uses the side-arm throw to start a double play (see page 25).

Clamp your throwing hand over the ball as quickly as possible.

2 Remove the ball from the glove. Bend your knees and take your arm back as you do so, so that you are ready to release the ball.

Basic throw

About 80 percent of fielders use this basic throwing motion. The arm should be over the top of the throw to help create efficient throwing mechanics and relieve stress on the throwing shoulder. Grip the ball across the seams, with the middle and index fingers on top of the ball and the thumb directly underneath.

Your body should be balanced before you begin the throw.

Take the ball out of the glove.

Turn your body sideways to your target.

Keep the elbow up to make your throw more controlled and accurate.

1 Bring the ball and glove into the chest. Place the tips of your middle and index fingers on the seams to get a good grip.

Your feet are apart and your legs are slightly bent.

2 Square off the pivot foot, so that the instep faces your target. Begin to move into a sideways position.

3 Bring the throwing arm down, back, and up. Point at your target with your non-throwing arm.

{ **Coming to grips** Do not hold the ball in the palm of your hand, because this will make it difficult to control when you throw it.

Your pivot foot squares aound to face your target.

our fingers hould be on p of the ll.

Perfect practice
Practice with a partner to perfect the correct techniques for both throwing and receiving.

Get the glove out of the way as you prepare to throw.

Flex your elbow.

Push off with the back foot.

Keep the back knee bent throughout this throw.

Release the ball in front of your body.

Your front foot remains firmly on the ground.

For this throw, your arm should be between your belt and your knees when you release the ball.

Open your fingers as you release the ball.

3 Keeping the body low, step toward your target. Make sure you have a good grip on the ball and that your eyes are focused in the direction of your throw.

4 Come forward in the direction that you want to throw and release the ball. Make sure your body stays low and your front foot is planted firmly on the ground.

5 Let your arm come down across your body as you follow through. Keep your knees bent to help you stay balanced.

4 Your hips and chest should now e facing your target. ush off with your ear foot to build p momentum r the throw.

se this arm to oint at your arget.

Look directly at your target as you throw.

5 Release the ball with a downward snap of the wrist. Your arm should continue coming forward after the release.

To help your follow-through, imagine that you are throwing your shoulder into the receiver's glove.

Release the ball in front of your body.

6 You must follow through after the release, or your throw will lose a lot of its speed and accuracy. Bring your arm down across your body and your back (or pivot) foot around. You should now be facing your target.

Your arm comes down at the end of the follow-through.

Push off with the rear (pivot) foot.

Both feet are parallel.

Fielding

THERE ARE NINE defensive positions in baseball – the pitcher, the catcher, first base, second base, shortstop, third base, left field, center field, and right field. Although each position requires different fielding skills, each player must master the fundamental techniques to be successful. These include always keeping the ball in front of you and learning how to field different types of ball.

Relaxed position

It is important that between pitches, when there are no runners on base or when time is out, players are able to relax. Baseball can be a long game and to stay in the ready position throughout the game would be too tiring. However, you should revert to the ready position as soon as the pitcher starts to deliver the pitch.

Place your hands on your knees for the relaxed position.

Your feet can be flat on the ground in this position.

Watch the ball so that you are ready to react as soon as it is hit.

Ready for action

Your ready position should be comfortable so that you can move easily and well. Adapt the basic ready position shown here to find one that suits you.

Your weight should be evenly distributed and you should be on the balls of your feet, ready to move in any direction.

Bend slightly at the waist.

The glove should be open, ready to field the ball.

Knees bent, ready to move.

Ready position

When the pitcher pitches the ball, all of the fielders will assume the ready position. Your feet should be shoulder-width apart, and your knees are bent. The hands should be out front, not on the knees, ready to field any ball that is hit.

Fielding a ground ball

When a ball is on the ground, your main priority is to stop it. Keep your body low and watch the ball until it is in the glove.

Try to get your body in front of the ball.

The glove is open, so that the ball can roll into it.

Your left foot is forward as you reach down with your glove.

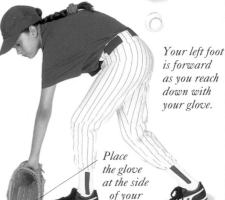

Place the glove at the side of your foot.

Backhanding the ball

When the ball is hit to your bare-hand side and is difficult to get in front of, you can backhand the ball. This involves reaching out to your backhand side to get the ball.

Getting to a nearby ground ball

Not all balls are hit directly toward a fielder, and you must be able to react and move toward a ball quickly so that you are in the correct fielding position. There are several ways to do this. Always ensure that your movements are controlled, so that you can successfully make the play.

Keep a good fielding position as you move.

Pivot on your back foot.

Your front leg crosses over your back leg.

Shuffle your feet from side to side.

Side step
Use a side step to get to a ball that is to the side of you or a short distance away. From the ready position, side step your feet toward the ball.

Crossover step
When you need to turn and run quickly over a longer distance, use the crossover step. Cross one foot over the other and run in the direction of the front foot.

Catching a direct ball

When a ball is heading directly toward you, try to watch it all the way into the glove, and catch it with two hands. Make sure your throwing hand is behind the glove. Soften the impact of the ball by relaxing your hands as you catch it.

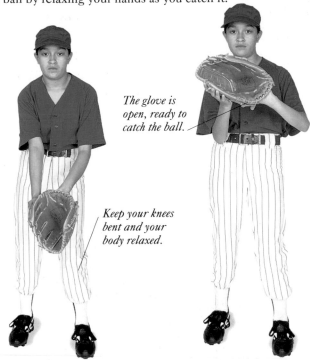

The glove is open, ready to catch the ball.

Keep your knees bent and your body relaxed.

1 When the ball is below the waist, your fingers should be pointing downward. Your little fingers are together and you should bring the ball in to your waist.

2 If the ball is above the waist, your fingers should be facing upward, with the thumbs together. Bring your hands in and up to chest level.

Sprinting to a ground ball

When a ball is hit farther away, you need to react quickly. Sprint after the ball so that you can field it as fast as possible.

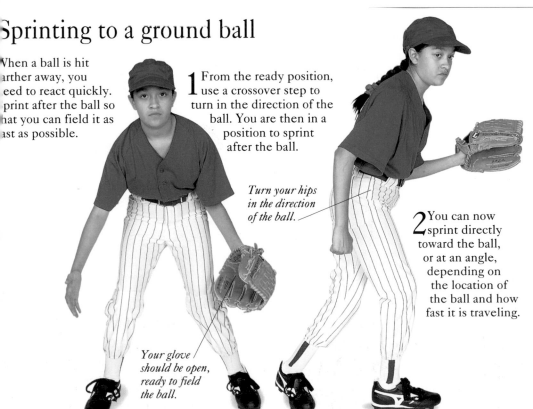

1 From the ready position, use a crossover step to turn in the direction of the ball. You are then in a position to sprint after the ball.

Turn your hips in the direction of the ball.

2 You can now sprint directly toward the ball, or at an angle, depending on the location of the ball and how fast it is traveling.

Your glove should be open, ready to field the ball.

As the ball comes into the glove, squeeze the ball to secure it.

Catch a fly ball above your head, in both hands.

Catching a fly ball
A fly ball is a ball that is hit high into the air. When you catch a fly ball, the batter is automatically out.

First and third bases

THE FIRST AND THIRD basemen are infielders. Their primary responsibility is to field the ball and stop the other team from scoring by getting them out. Both cover the areas around their respective bases, but position themselves so that if the ball is hit away from them, they can comfortably get to their base to receive a throw. They stand 6–13 ft (2–4 m) from the base, in fair territory. This increases their fielding range, enabling them to field a fair ball to their right or left.

Playing the base

Once the ball has been hit away from you at first base, position yourself at the base. Have your right foot on the inside of the base and be in a relaxed position so that you can receive the ball. This position is important, because it allows you to react quickly to any bad throws.

The glove should be open and relaxed, ready to receive the ball.

In position
Get to the base as quickly as possible. Do not stretch too early or try to predict where the throw will be. Be ready to field the ball wherever it is thrown.

First baseman

As a first baseman, you have to catch and field balls hit to the first base area, and get runners out by touching (tagging) first base. It is therefore vital that you can handle different kinds of throw.

Your right foot should stay on the inside of the base so that the runner can run over the outside of the base.

1 For a direct throw, get to the base, turn toward the fielder, and hold your glove up as a target.

2 As the ball comes toward you, keep one foot on the base and stretch to catch it.

Blocking the ball

As first baseman, you have to block any bad throws. If the ball gets past you, the runner will be able to advance to second and even third base. Drop to your knees and get behind the ball, blocking it with your body.

1 If the ball is thrown to your left, step to your left to field it.

Move your right foot to the corner of the base.

Reach for the ball.

2 The step should keep you inside the baseline, to avoid a collision with the incoming runner.

Keep your right foot on the corner of the base.

Ball in the dirt

You will regularly have to field balls that are thrown in front of you into the dirt. These are very difficult to field, and you must learn to scoop the ball into your glove to make the play.

Your glove should be open, ready to receive the ball.

Squeeze the ball as it enters your glove.

1 If the ball is thrown to your right, step to your right, across your body, to field it.

2 Step into the flight of the ball, stretching to catch it as soon as possible.

Make sure the glove is open and positioned in the dirt, so that the ball can enter the glove.

Place your right foot on the back corner of the base.

Stay low
Get as low to the ground as possible. Try not to let the ball bounce, and if it does, try to catch it on the bounce.

Holding runners

When there is a runner on first base, you will have to hold the runner close to the base. This will prevent him from getting a big lead, and make it more difficult for him to steal second base. In most instances, you should position yourself on the base, ready to receive a throw from the pitcher.

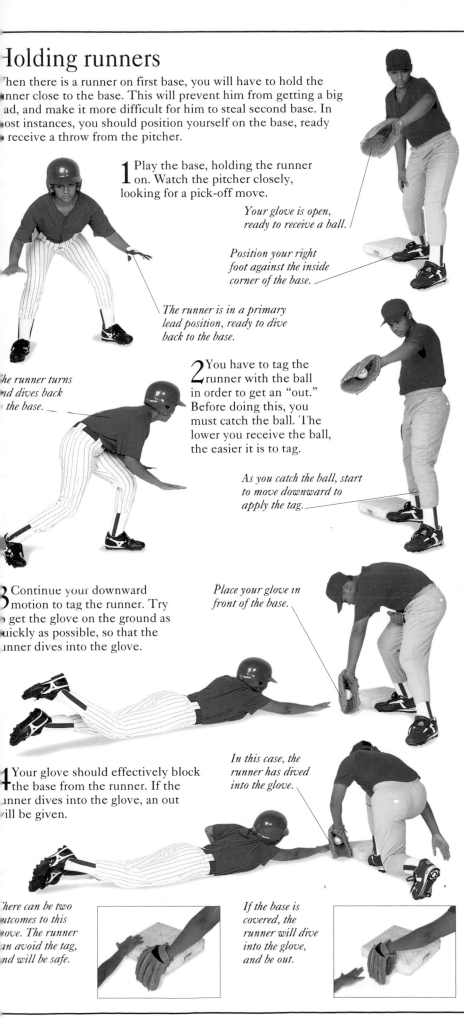

1 Play the base, holding the runner on. Watch the pitcher closely, looking for a pick-off move.

Your glove is open, ready to receive a ball.

Position your right foot against the inside corner of the base.

The runner is in a primary lead position, ready to dive back to the base.

The runner turns and dives back to the base.

2 You have to tag the runner with the ball in order to get an "out." Before doing this, you must catch the ball. The lower you receive the ball, the easier it is to tag.

As you catch the ball, start to move downward to apply the tag.

3 Continue your downward motion to tag the runner. Try to get the glove on the ground as quickly as possible, so that the runner dives into the glove.

Place your glove in front of the base.

4 Your glove should effectively block the base from the runner. If the runner dives into the glove, an out will be given.

In this case, the runner has dived into the glove.

There can be two outcomes to this move. The runner can avoid the tag, and will be safe.

If the base is covered, the runner will dive into the glove, and be out.

Third base

Third base is known as the "hot corner" because many hard-hit balls are directed here. As third baseman, you will sometimes have to make the longest throw across the diamond to first, and must therefore have a strong throwing arm.

In a potential bunt situation, position yourself close to third base.

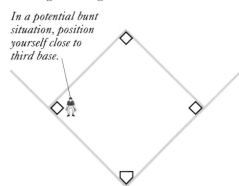

Playing close

In a potential bunt situation, that is one with less than two outs and runners on first, or runners on first and second, you must be prepared to play in. This makes it difficult for the batter to bunt successfully. Be prepared for him to swing normally, too.

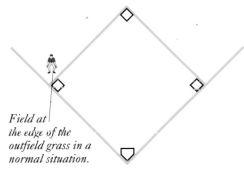

Field at the edge of the outfield grass in a normal situation.

Normal depth

In a normal situation, with no runners on base, or with two outs, you can field your position at normal depth. This means you are about halfway to the edge of the outfield grass, which will give you greater fielding range, and more time to field the ball.

Bare-handed pick up

In certain situations, such as a bunt or a slow roller, the play has to be made in a hurry. You do not have time to field the ball into your glove. Instead, you will have to field the ball in your bare hand and make a quick throw to first base.

Second base

SECOND BASE IS A BUSY position. The second baseman is responsible for a large area, and must be quick and agile. Much of his role involves fielding the ball quickly and cleanly and making good, strong, accurate throws. He is also, along with the shortstop, responsible for initiating and turning double plays and tagging out any runners trying to steal second base.

Initiating a double play

A double play is when the defense gets two outs on one hit ball. If the ball is hit between first and second base, and there is a runner on first base, you should field the ball and initiate a double play by throwing to the shortstop, who will be covering second base.

1 To start a double play, get into a good fielding position directly behind the ball. Stay low, watching the ball all the way into the glove.

Get a good grip on the ball as you prepare to throw it.

2 Transfer the ball quickly to your throwing hand. Drop to one knee and pivot toward second base

3 On one knee, take the arm back into a good throwing position.

Throwing arm follows through.

4 Throw the ball over the base. The ball should be in a good position for the shortstop to touch second base and throw the ball to first base. This is called turning a double play.

Taking a throw from the catcher

When there is a right-handed batter at the plate and a runner at first base tries to steal second base, it is the second baseman's responsibility to cover second base. Most right-handed batters will pull the ball to the left-hand side of the infield. It therefore makes sense for the second baseman to break for the base, to receive the throw from the catcher.

1 As soon as the runner goes, run directly to the base and straddle it. Hold the glove open, ready to receive the ball.

Clamp the ball firmly in the glove.

Hold the glove open, ready to receive the ball.

Place one foot on either side of the base.

2 Keep your eyes on the ball as you catch it with two hands. Clamp the ball into the glove with your bare hand.

Hand in glove
Keep your hand inside your glove to protect it and to ensure that you do not drop the ball.

Bend your knees so that you are firmly balanced as you receive the ball.

22

Throw to one side

A throw from the catcher, trying to throw out a base stealer, can often be off target. In these situations, the second baseman's priority is to get to the ball and make the tag.

2 Start to lean over the base and bring the glove downward, ready to make the tag.

Catch the ball with two hands.

3 Apply the tag, in a one-handed sweeping motion with the glove closed.

1 Get in line with the throw, make sure you are balanced, and catch the ball in the middle of your body, with two hands.

Your foot should be next to the base.

{ Easy does it
It is easier to stretch and reach the base with a one-handed tag.

This is called a one-handed tag.

Making the tag

If you place the glove directly in front of the base, the base runner will have no way of getting to the base. If he slides into the glove, he is out.

Look down at the base as you prepare to make the tag.

{ Covering the steal
Don't stretch for the incoming runner, let him slide into the glove and tag himself. As soon as the tag is made, bring your glove back up and show it to the umpire.

3 After you have received the ball, start to bend your knees to get lower to the base and sweep downward with your hands.

Your glove should be in front of the base.

4 Place your glove in front of the base, so that the runner will slide directly into the glove and be out.

Turning a double play

If the batter hits the ball between second and third bases, the shortstop will field the ball and throw it to the second baseman. You have to catch the ball and make a quick throw to first base to throw the runner out.

1 Break toward second base, with your hands out ready to receive the throw.

Transfer the ball to your throwing hand.

2 Catch the ball with two hands, and step onto second base as you transfer the ball to your throwing hand.

Step onto the base.

3 Use the base to pivot around toward first base and step forward.

Pivot on this foot.

Step toward first base with this foot.

4 Release the ball as quickly as you can. Be ready to avoid the base runner, who will be sliding into second base.

Make sure you follow through after the throw.

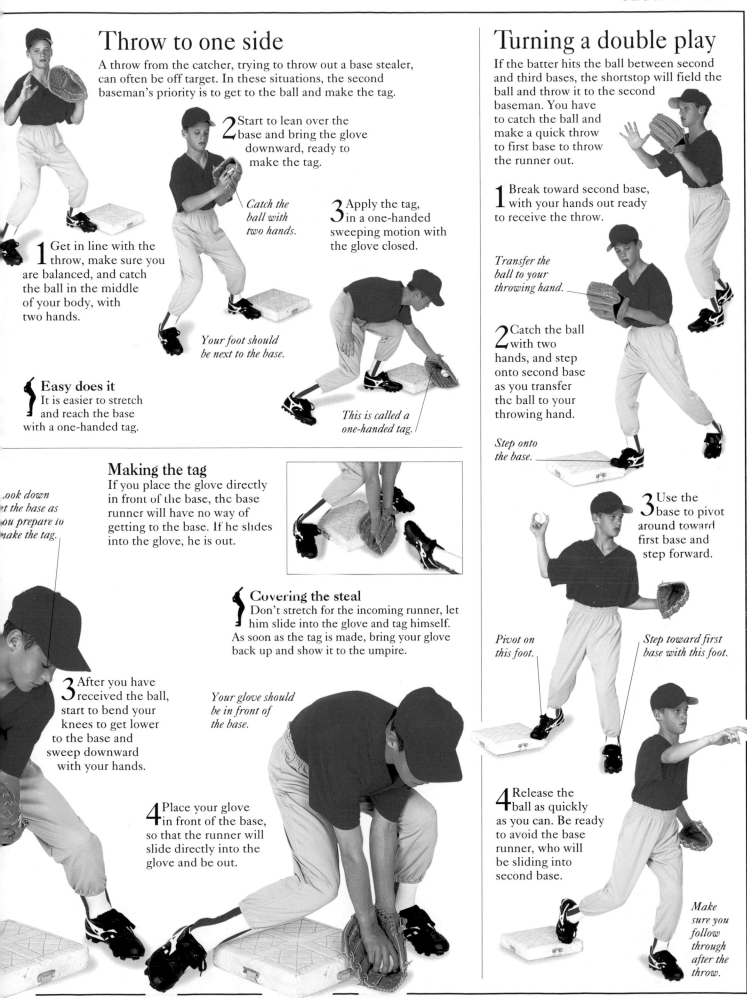

Shortstop

THE BALL IS hit to shortstop more often than any other player on the field, making this a very important position. The shortstop needs a strong, accurate throwing arm to make long throws to first base, and quick, agile feet to avoid sliding runners on a double-play pivot.

Let the ball rest momentarily in your fingers before you throw.

Keep your arm low after you release the ball.

Your feet should be on either side of the ball.

Step toward the base.

Ball hit to the left

If the ball is hit to the left of the shortstop with a runner on first base, your first priority is to field the ball. It is then a short throw to force the runner out at second base.

1 Side step or shuffle so that you are directly behind the ball. Field the ball and transfer it quickly to your throwing hand.

2 Stay low and step toward second base. Use an underarm throw to toss the ball to the second baseman.

3 After you have thrown, continue on your path toward the base. Keep your body low.

Turning a double play

In this situation, the shortstop receives the ball from the second baseman, touches second base to force the runner out, then throws the ball to first base to turn a double play.

Teamwork
The shortstop and second baseman must work as a team and communicate during this play, so that it is as smooth and as quick as possible.

2 Step onto second base as you transfer the ball to your throwing hand. Focus on making the throw, not on the incoming runner. If you step on the base before the runner arrives, the runner is out.

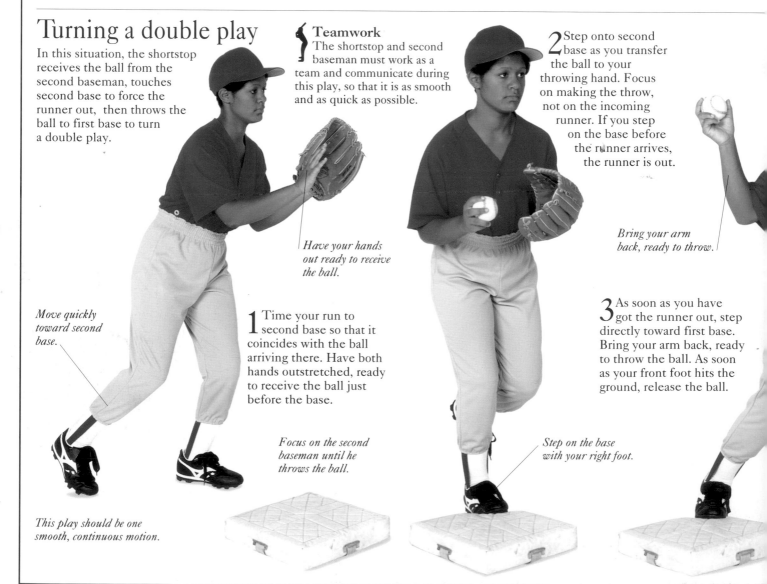

Have your hands out ready to receive the ball.

Bring your arm back, ready to throw.

Move quickly toward second base.

1 Time your run to second base so that it coincides with the ball arriving there. Have both hands outstretched, ready to receive the ball just before the base.

Focus on the second baseman until he throws the ball.

3 As soon as you have got the runner out, step directly toward first base. Bring your arm back, ready to throw the ball. As soon as your front foot hits the ground, release the ball.

Step on the base with your right foot.

This play should be one smooth, continuous motion.

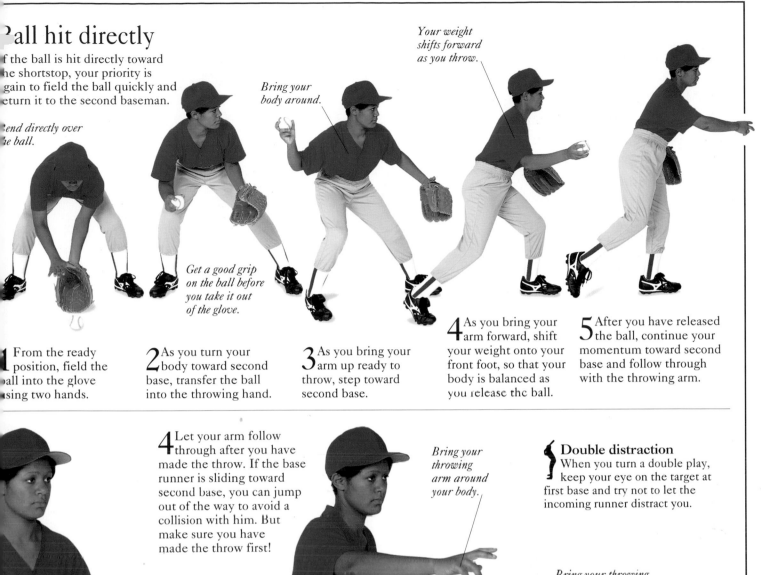

Ball hit directly

If the ball is hit directly toward the shortstop, your priority is again to field the ball quickly and return it to the second baseman.

Bend directly over the ball.

Bring your body around.

Your weight shifts forward as you throw.

Get a good grip on the ball before you take it out of the glove.

1 From the ready position, field the ball into the glove using two hands.

2 As you turn your body toward second base, transfer the ball into the throwing hand.

3 As you bring your arm up ready to throw, step toward second base.

4 As you bring your arm forward, shift your weight onto your front foot, so that your body is balanced as you release the ball.

5 After you have released the ball, continue your momentum toward second base and follow through with the throwing arm.

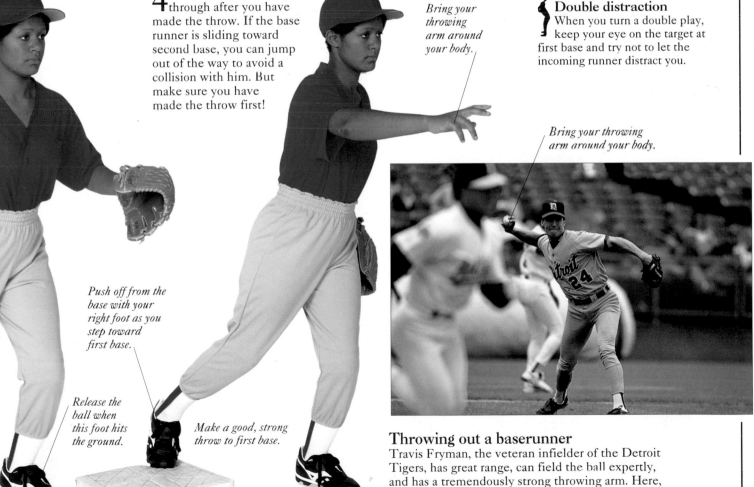

4 Let your arm follow through after you have made the throw. If the base runner is sliding toward second base, you can jump out of the way to avoid a collision with him. But make sure you have made the throw first!

Bring your throwing arm around your body.

Double distraction
When you turn a double play, keep your eye on the target at first base and try not to let the incoming runner distract you.

Bring your throwing arm around your body.

Push off from the base with your right foot as you step toward first base.

Release the ball when this foot hits the ground.

Make a good, strong throw to first base.

Throwing out a baserunner
Travis Fryman, the veteran infielder of the Detroit Tigers, has great range, can field the ball expertly, and has a tremendously strong throwing arm. Here, Travis is about to throw out the baserunner. Note how his eyes are fixed on the target as he prepares to release the ball.

Pitching and grips

T**HE PITCHER IS** vital to the team's defense and success. He (or she) puts the ball into play, and tries to prevent the other team from scoring by making the batter hit a ball that can be fielded for an out. A good pitcher will be able to throw different kinds of pitches to deceive the batter and can be trained to throw the ball exactly where he wants to. This forces the batter to hit the ball in a certain way.

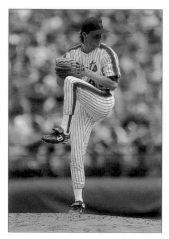

Ready to pitch
Jeff Innis of the New York Mets in the tuck position just before he pitches the ball.

Lean forwards slightly.

Pitching from the wind-up position

The wind-up position helps you generate momentum and throw the ball with greater speed. It should be used when there are no runners on base.

Keep the ball inside the glove so that the batter cannot see it.

Make sure you get a good grip on the ball.

This knee should be slightly flexed.

Your hips should be square, and your body facing the batter.

The inside of this leg faces home plate.

Nonpivot foot

Pivot foot

The batter will see the back of the glove, not the ball.

1 Place one or both feet on the rubber of the pitching mound, get the signal from the catcher, and adjust your grip accordingly.

2 Start the wind-up sequence by stepping back with your non-pivot foot (here the left foot).

3 Turn the pivot (right) foot sideways along the rubber, so that your instep is facing the batter.

4 Bring the nonpivot leg through into a coil position. Try to stay balanced with your body in a tucked position, so that you can then explode into the pitch.

et position

hen there are runners on base, the
tcher uses the set position. This forces
y base runners to stay closer to the base,
d makes it harder for them to steal a
se. From the set position, you can either
tch the ball, throw to a base, or step off
e pitching rubber.

*From the rubber,
look at the catcher
to receive his signal
before moving into
the set position.*

*From the set position,
drive your body
toward home plate
to pitch the ball.*

Grips

A pitcher uses different grips to give a ball spin, or to make it travel in a straight or curved line. You can also use grips to change the speed of the ball in the air, which is a good way to deceive a batter.

*For a four-seam
fastball, grip
the ball across the
seams. This ball
will travel through
the air in a
straight line.*

Flight of the four-seam fastball from above

*For a two-seam
fastball, grip the
ball along the seams.
When thrown, this
ball may move
in the air.*

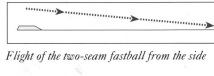

Flight of the two-seam fastball from the side

*For a curve ball,
grip the ball with one
finger along the
seams and the other
next to it. Spin the
ball out of your hand
as you throw it.*

Flight of the curve ball from above

*For the
change-up,
hold the
ball in the
back of the hand. In the
air, this ball looks like
a fastball, but is slower.*

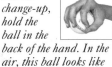

Flight of the change up from the side

*Release the ball in
front of the body.*

*The front arm
pushes down
and away*

*Stride
toward
home plate.*

*ur throwing
m comes
wn, back,
d up as you
epare to pitch.*

*Hips come
around.*

*Bring your back
foot forward
to help you
balance.*

*Make sure you
follow through
after the release.*

Energy saver
Remember that
the pitching
action should be
smooth and efficient,
so that all of your
energy can be used
to pitch the ball.

5 Drive forward
using the pivot
leg. Your hands split
as you take your
throwing arm back,
ready to pitch.

6 Bring your hips around
to add more power to your
throwing arm. As you prepare
to release the ball, focus on
your target. Release the
ball out in front of you.

7 Once you have thrown
the ball, your arm should
follow through across your
body. This action makes
the arm slow down naturally
and helps prevent injury.

Catching

In this position, you will be able to handle any kind of pitch.

Hold the glove open to the pitcher so that he has a big target.

T HE CATCHER HAS possibly the toughest position in baseball. The catcher must be quick, agile, and strong, and have a good throwing arm. He also needs to be a leader in the field because he calls all the pitches through a series of signals with the pitcher, and his team depends on him to make the correct decisions. The catcher must be ready for any offensive plays, and should know the strengths, weaknesses, and tendencies of each batter so he can decide what pitch to signal.

Catcher's signals
A catcher has a set of signals that tell the pitcher which pitch to throw. From the crouch position, hold a set number of fingers between your legs. One finger usually means a fastball, two a curve ball, and so on.

Make sure the opposition cannot see your signals.

Catcher's stance
Once you have given your signal, you can assume the catcher's stance. This should be a comfortable position that is as low as possible to give the umpire a good view of the plate.

Make sure your body is balanced.

Legs wide apart.

Catching pop-ups
A ball that is "popped up" directly behind the catcher by a batter goes very high into the air and has a lot of spin on it. As a catcher, it is important that you can catch these balls, because they are easy outs.

Get your mask off quickly.

1 As soon as the ball is popped up, get up out of your stance and locate its position.

Turn toward the ball.

2 As soon as you locate the ball, throw your mask in the opposite direction and move quickly to catch the ball.

Throwing out base runners
When there are runners on base, one of the catcher's jobs is to throw out any base stealers. If you can do this well, it is unlikely that the runners will try to steal very often. However, you do need to be alert to this possibility, and should know the correct techniques for avoiding it.

Watch out for any base runners.

1 From the crouch position, receive the ball as usual.

Protect your throwing hand by keeping it behind your back.

Your weight is forward on the balls of your feet.

Step forward with your right leg.

Bring your throwing hand up so that you can remove the ball from the glove.

2 As soon as you catch the ball, drive up out of the catcher's box toward second or third base.

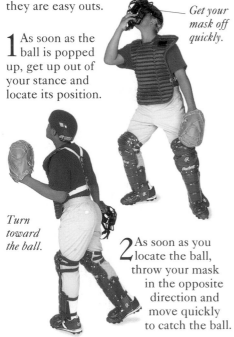
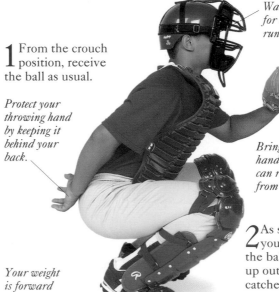

Outside the strike zone

As a catcher, you must be able to adjust to pitches that are not in the strike zone. Here are some examples of what to expect and how to react in such situations.

1 For a low pitch, rotate your mitt so that your fingers are pointing downward.

2 To catch a pitch to your right, extend your arm across your body. Have the glove facing outward.

3 To catch a pitch to your left, rotate your mitt so that your fingers are pointing upward.

Tag plays

When a runner is coming home to score a run, the catcher usually has to try to tag the runner to get him out. Collisions and injuries can occur, so make sure you get your technique correct.

1 As the ball approaches, get yourself into a good position, allowing the runner to see the back part of home plate.

Your knees should align directly with the foul line.

Let the runner see part of the plate.

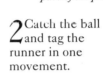

2 Catch the ball and tag the runner in one movement.

Block the plate and apply the tag.

Blocking the ball

When the pitcher throws the ball into the dirt during a game, the catcher must block it. If the ball gets past the catcher, any base runners may advance.

Slide in the direction of the ball.

1 If the ball is to the side, you have to move and block at the same time.

Place the glove in between your legs.

Drop to your knees quickly.

2 If the ball is directly in front, drop to your knees and let it bounce up into the chest protector.

3 Get a good grip on the ball as quickly as you can, so that you can make the throw.

Look directly at the base.

4 Continue driving toward second or third base as you make a good, strong throw in that direction.

Fast and furious
This is a very quick sequence and your throw must be fast and accurate to be effective.

Bring the glove down out of the way of your throw.

Drive with the back leg.

Follow through across the body.

5 Release the ball and follow through. Make sure you are ready in case there is another play.

The outfield

THE OUTFIELD positions are difficult and challenging to play. There are three outfielders and they have to defend a massive area. They also have to be able to maintain their concentration for long periods of time because most of the game takes place in the infield. As an outfielder you have to catch fly balls, field ground balls, and back up the infielders.

Outfield agility
Outfielder Reggie Sanders of the Cincinnati Reds makes a spectacular catch during a game at Wrigley Field, home of the Chicago Cubs.

Fielding a ground ball
When the outfielder has no play, for example when the batter has hit a sure single with no one on base, the outfielder should get into a long barrier position ready to field the ball. Get your body behind the ball and drop to one knee.

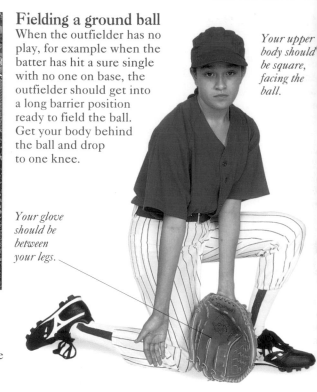

Your upper body should be square, facing the ball.

Your glove should be between your legs.

Do-or-die ground ball

When there is a chance that a runner might score, but a good throw could get him out, the outfielder should attempt a do-or-die play. This means that you have to field the ball at full speed, quickly transfer it to your throwing hand, and accurately make the throw back to the infield.

1 Approach the ball directly by running straight toward it at speed. Try to keep your movements controlled.

Bend your legs so that your body is low.

Your glove is open, ready to scoop the ball.

Remember you need a good grip before you throw the ball.

Your feet will be moving at speed toward the ball.

Taking a risk
Only use a do-or-die play in critical situations. You are fielding the ball with one hand and if it bounces oddly you can't block it with your body.

2 Field the ball slightly to the glove side. Keep your body low and scoop the ball into the glove.

Scoop the ball up into the glove.

Blocking the Sun

The Sun can be a real nuisance to an outfielder. However, you can use your glove to block out its rays so that you can still keep your eye on the ball.

Never look directly at the Sun; always shield your eyes from its rays.

Support

Whenever possible, get into position to back up another fielder. You will be in position to pick up the ball if he misses the catch.

The drop step

The ball is often hit over an outfielder's head. Instead of running backward to receive it, which is slow and awkward, you should do a short drop-back step and run after it. Try to judge where the ball will land, then head for that spot.

2 Bring your leg in front of you and run. Look back occasionally to keep your eyes on the ball.

Turn as quickly as possible.

1 Figure out which way the ball is traveling. Turn and get ready to start running in that direction.

Pick up the flight of the ball before you start running.

3 Keep traveling forward at speed as you field the ball and transfer it to your throwing hand.

Get a good grip on the ball before you take it out of the glove.

Running gives you momentum for a strong throw.

4 Keep driving toward the target as you pull the arm back, ready to throw the ball. If you are successful, the base runner will be out.

Your arm is back, ready to throw.

Bring the glove toward you as you get your body into a sideways position.

Outfield tactics

When you play the outfield, you must always throw the ball to the cut-off man. The cut-off man is an infielder, who can then relay the ball to any base to make a play. Here, Todd Zeile of the Baltimore Orioles relays the ball across the infield to throw out a baserunner.

Hitting and bunting

TO BE A SUCCESSFUL hitter, you need good hand-eye coordination, speed, power, and awareness. Hitting a fast-pitched, round ball with a round bat is a very difficult skill to master, and even the best hitters in the major leagues only hit the ball successfully three times in ten attempts. Master the basic techniques for batting, then try to find your own style.

Hitting the ball

There are three main stages in the batting swing: the stride, the swing, and the follow-through. You need to be aggressive and want to hit the ball as hard as possible, while still maintaining your form.

1 Get into a position where your bat covers the whole of the plate when you swing.

Touch the outside corner of home plate with the tip of your bat.

A batting glove will give you more grip.

3 Take a small step forward with the left leg as you start your swing. This is the stride. It should be a smooth, deliberate, movement, rather than a quick lunge forward.

Step forward with this leg.

Shake on it
To help you master the correct grip, imagine you are shaking hands with the bat.

4 As you bring your hands forward, your back foot pivots. Keep your eyes on the ball at all times and bring your hands directly toward it.

Pivot on your back foot.

Your hands should be together at the base of the bat.

Feet shoulder-width apart.

The grip
The bat should feel comfortable in your hands. Hold it firmly, and try to align the middle joints of the top hand with the knuckles of the bottom hand.

2 Place your feet shoulder-width apart, with your knees slightly bent and your eyes looking directly ahead at the pitcher. This is the correct batting stance, but you can alter it slightly so that it is comfortable for you.

Hitting in style
Eduardo Perez shows immense concentration as he keeps his eye on the ball, ready to explode through it when it makes contact with his bat.

As you wait for the pitch, your grip should be firm but relaxed to prevent tension in your arms and shoulders.

Bring your elbows down.

32

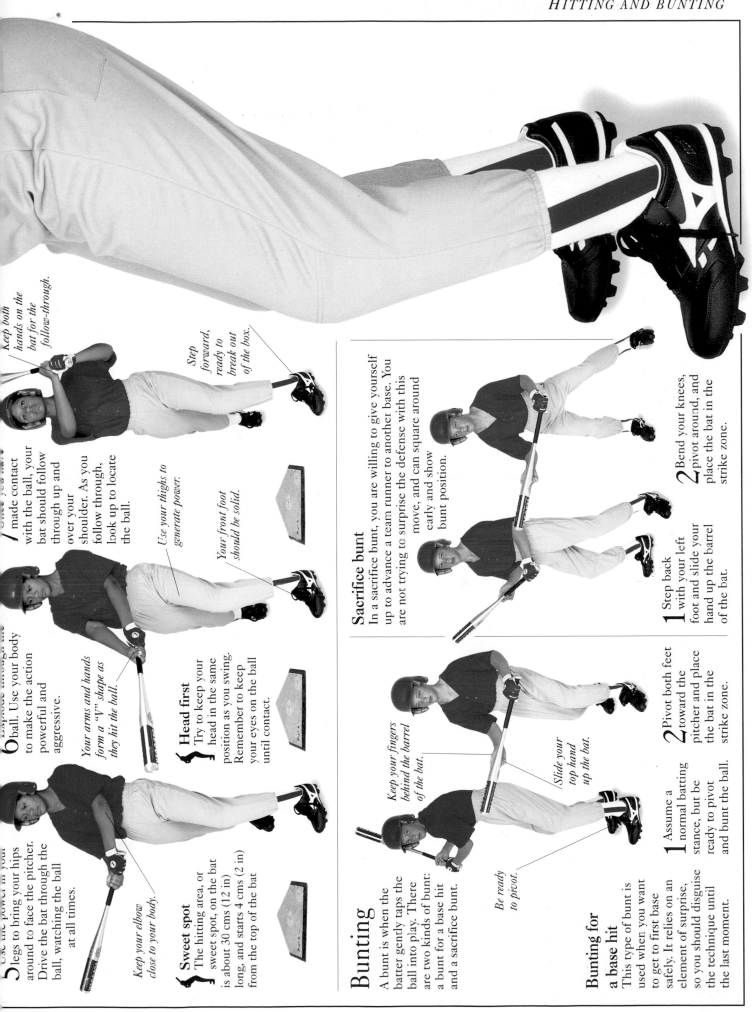

Keep both hands on the bat for the follow-through.

Step forward, ready to break out of the box.

7 Once you have made contact with the ball, your bat should follow through up and over your shoulder. As you follow through, look up to locate the ball.

Use your thighs to generate power.

Your front foot should be solid.

6 Explode through the ball. Use your body to make the action powerful and aggressive.

Your arms and hands form a "V" shape as they hit the ball.

} Head first
Try to keep your head in the same position as you swing. Remember to keep your eyes on the ball until contact.

5 Use the power in your legs to bring your hips around to face the pitcher. Drive the bat through the ball, watching the ball at all times.

Keep your elbow close to your body.

} Sweet spot
The hitting area, or sweet spot, on the bat is about 30 cms (12 in) long, and starts 4 cms (2 in) from the top of the bat

Bunting

A bunt is when the batter gently taps the ball into play. There are two kinds of bunt: a bunt for a base hit and a sacrifice bunt.

Bunting for a base hit

This type of bunt is used when you want to get to first base safely. It relies on an element of surprise, so you should disguise the technique until the last moment.

Keep your fingers behind the barrel of the bat.

Slide your top hand up the bat.

1 Assume a normal batting stance, but be ready to pivot and bunt the ball.

Be ready to pivot.

2 Pivot both feet toward the pitcher and place the bat in the strike zone.

Sacrifice bunt

In a sacrifice bunt, you are willing to give yourself up to advance a team runner to another base. You are not trying to surprise the defense with this move, and can square around early and show bunt position.

1 Step back with your left foot and slide your hand up the barrel of the bat.

2 Bend your knees, pivot around, and place the bat in the strike zone.

Baserunning

AS SOON AS THE BATTER puts the ball into play, he becomes a base runner. Good baserunning can often win games, but you should remember that poor baserunning can lead to the defensive team getting easy outs. As a base runner, you need to be alert and ready for anything. You can advance around the bases on hits from your team-mates, bunts, passed balls, wild pitches, and overthrows and you can also steal bases.

Breaking out of the box

Once you have put the ball into play, you have to get on the base as quickly as possible. Immediately after contact, you must break out of the batter's box and head toward first base.

1 Make sure you are in a good position to hit the ball (see pages 32-33). As it approaches you, drive it out into play in front of you.

Grip the bat firmly with both hands.

Look up at the ball for a couple of steps if it is in the infield. Always listen to the base coach for advice.

2 Follow through your swing after contact. Let go of the bat with your top hand. At the same time, angle your body toward first base, ready to start running.

Only your left hand should be on the bat at this stage.

3 As you start running, drop the bat to the ground, but do not throw it.

Keep looking forward as you let go of the bat behind you.

Use your feet to drive out of the box.

4 After you have dropped the bat, keep your body low and drive with your legs to get up to full running speed. Run directly toward first base, in the running alley along the baseline.

Between the lines
When you run from home plate to first base you have to run between the foul line and the line that runs outside and parallel to it, or you will be out.

Tagging up

When you are on second or third base and a fly ball is hit, stay on the base until the ball is caught. Then you can judge whether to run on to the next base, or tag up.

Keep your heel on the front edge of the base until you move on.

Breaking out of the box

As soon as he has hit the ball, Brian Jordan of the St Louis Cardinals explodes out of the box toward first base.

Advancing on a ground ball

If a ground ball is hit to your left while you are on second base, and there are no other runners on base, you should try to advance. Angle your body away from the base so that you are in a good position to sprint to the next one.

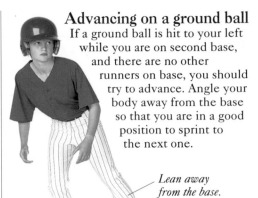

Lean away from the base.

Running through first

First base is the only base you can overrun without being tagged out. Sprint through the base, touching the nearest part of it. Lean into the base as you run.

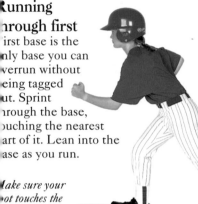

Make sure your foot touches the front edge of the base.

Rounding first

If you want to run more than one base, run in a curve, which is quicker. Lean away from the base as you pass it.

Touch the inside part of the base, using it to drive toward the next base.

Freezing on a ground ball

If the ball is hit to your right and you are not forced to move, you should freeze. Be ready to return to your base if necessary.

Place your weight on your back foot, ready to return.

Taking the lead

If you are on first base during a fly ball, take a good lead toward second base. If the ball is dropped, you may be able to advance to third base.

Sliding

You cannot overrun second or third base. The quickest way to stop at these bases is therefore to slide. Sliding is also a good way to avoid a tag. Try to slide on the side of your left foot and buttocks, keeping your hands well out of the way and your right foot off the ground to avoid injury.

Sliding to safety

A player for the Toronto Blue Jays slides in to second base. The Blue Jays won back-to-back World Series Championships in 1992 and 1993.

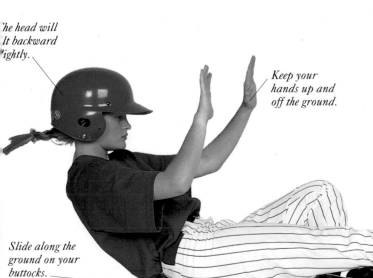

The head will tilt backward slightly.

Keep your hands up and off the ground.

Slide along the ground on your buttocks.

Keep your front foot off the ground as you slide into the base, to avoid injury.

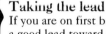

Taking it further

ONCE YOU HAVE mastered the basic techniques involved in playing baseball, you may decide that you want to take the sport further. One of the biggest sports programms in the world is Little League Baseball, which girls and boys up to the age of 18 years can take part in. From here, you may want to progress to amateur baseball or even to the professional minor and major leagues.

Little League world series
Every year at Williamsport, Pennsylvania, eight teams compete to win the Little League world series. This series is for players aged 11-12, and attracts the best teams from all over the world. Here, the US East team is congratulating teammate Craig Stinson for hitting a home run.

The Atlanta Olympics.
Since 1992, baseball has been a full medal sport in the Olympic Games. At the 1996 Olympic Games in Atlanta, Georgia, US, the final was between Cuba and Japan. In recent years, Cuba has dominated amateur and Olympic baseball, and won the gold medal here with a score of 13–9. Japan won the silver medal and the US won the bronze.

American Olympics
The US Olympic baseball team is made up of college players. However, at the 2000 Olympics in Sydney, Australia, it has been decided that professionals can play.

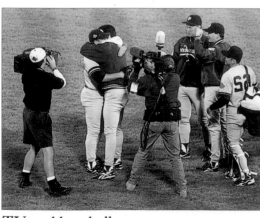

TV and baseball
Many of the large baseball events, such as the World Series, attract international press and television coverage. Here, John Wetteland and Andy Pettitte celebrate the New York Yankees' victory over the Atlanta Braves in 1996.

World Series trophy
The prestigious World Series has been played since 1905. Today, the winning teams from the Eastern and Western Divisions of major league teams meet to battle it out for the coveted trophy.

Glossary

Ball Ball thrown by the pitcher which is judged to be outside the strike zone.
Base hit Batter hits the ball into fair territory and gets on base safely.
Bases loaded Runners on all the bases.
Bull pen Area where pitchers warm up before pitching.
Caught stealing Runner gets thrown out by catcher while attempting to steal a base.
Double Batter gets base hit and reaches second base safely.
Double play Batting team gets two outs in succession (on the same play).
Error A fielding mistake that would otherwise have put a runner out.
Fair ball A ball that is hit into fair territory
Fair territory The area of the field between the first and third baselines.
Fastball A pitch that is thrown as fast as possible.
Fly ball A ball that is hit high in the air towards the outfield.
Foul ball A ball that does not go into fair territory.
Foul territory The area of the field that i outside the first and third baselines.
Full count Pitcher throws three balls and two strikes.
Grand slam Batter hits home run with the bases loaded.
Hit Batter reaches base after hitting successfully.
Home run Batter hits a fair ball over the outfield fence and completes a circuit, touching all the bases without stopping.
Inning An inning is complete when both teams have batted once.
Line drive Batter hits ball hard and level.
Pop up Batter hits ball high into the air, and it is caught by an infielder.
Run A run is scored when a runner touches all the bases in the correct order.
Sacrifice bunt Batter sacrifices self by bunting to advance runner to the next available base.
Sacrifice fly Batter sacrifices self with lon fly ball, which is caught, to advance runner.
Single Batter gets base hit and reaches first base safely.
Stolen base Runner successfully runs to next available base during pitch.
Strike Ball thrown by the pitcher which is judged to be in the strike zone.
Strike out When the batter has three strike
Strike zone Zone over home plate above the knees and below the chest of the batter.
Triple Batter gets base hit and reaches thir base safely.
Triple play Three outs in succession.
Wild pitch Ball thrown which cannot be caught by catcher.

Index

A
dvancing on a ground ball 35
nson, Adrian "Cap" 9

B
abe Ruth 9
all 11
all in the dirt 20
are-handed pick up 21
ase running 34
ats 11
locking the ball 20, 29
locking the Sun 31
reaking out of the box 34
unting 32–33

C
atcher's stance 28
atching 28
Cincinnati Red Stockings 9
leats 10
overing the steal 23
rossover step 19
urved turn 35

D, E
irect ball 19
o-or-die ground ball 30
ouble play 22, 23, 24
rop step 31
quipment 10–11

F
ielder's glove 11
ielding 18
ielding a ground ball 18
ield positions 14
irst base 20
irst baseman 20
y ball 19
oul lines 14, 15
reezing on a ground ball 35

G, H
grips 26–27
ground ball 19, 35
helmets 11
hitting 32–33
holding runners 21
home plate

I
infield 14, 15

M
making the tag 23

N, O, P
near ground ball 19
officials 14
outfield 30, 31
pitching 26–27
pop-ups 28

R, S
ready position 18
second base 22, 23
set position 27
short stop 24, 25
signals (catcher) 28
sliding 35
stealing bases 28, 35
stirrups 10

T
tagging up 35
tag plays 29
third base 20, 21
throwing 16

U, W
undershirt 10
uniform 10, 11
warming up 12–13
wind-up position 26

Useful addresses

Major League Baseball
350 Park Avenue,
New York, NY 10022
Tel: 212/339-7800

USA Baseball (Olympic)
2160 Greenwood Avenue
Trenton, NJ 08609
Tel: 609/586-2381

**Little League Baseball
Incorporated**
P.O. Box 3485
Williamsport, PA 17701

**American Baseball Coaches
Association**
108 South University Avenue
Suite 3
Mount Pleasant, MI 48858–2327

Baseball Hall of Fame
Box 590
Cooperstown, NY 13326
Tel: 607/547-7200

Baseball Canada
208-1600 James Naismith Avenue
Gloucester, Ontario
K1B 5N4
Tel: (613) 748-5606
website: www.baseball.ca

Baseball Ontario
1425 Bishop St. N., #16
Cambridge, Ontario
N1R 6J9
Tel: (519) 740-3900

Acknowledgments

DK would like to thank the following people for their help in the production of this book:

pecial thanks to Jorge Fredericks of the merican Little League and Paul Vernon f the British Baseball Federation for their echnical advice and help in organizing the hoto shoots; all the young baseball players or their patience and enthusiasm during he photography; Rob Butler and Charles Henderson of Cincinnati Reds Public Relations for liaising with Eduardo Perez and he Reds; Dave Phillips and the staff and upils at Easthampstead Park School, Bracknell, for their cooperation and nthusiasm; Rawlings for the catcher's quipment; Louisville Slugger for the gloves; Spartan Sports for supplying the uniforms and equipment; Nichola Roberts for editorial assistance; Goldberry Broad for design assistance; Joe Hoyle for the jacket design.

Picture credits
The publisher would like to thank the following for their kind permission to reproduce the photographs:
Key: *b* bottom, *c* centre, *l* left, *r* right, *t* top,
Allsport USA: Al Bello *36tc*, Otto Creule *8br*, Jonathan Daniel *8tr*, *30tc*, *35tc*, Stephen Dunn *8c*, Jed Jacobsohn *25bl*, Doug Pensinger *31bc*, *36bl*, *bc*, Todd Warshaw *32tr*, **Archive**

Photos: Reuters: JT Lovette *8bl*, John Sommers *8cl*, Ray Stubblebine *10bl*; **Colorsport:** Focus-West *15bl*, **Corbis-Bettmann:** *9tl*, *cl*, *cr*, *bl*, *br*; **Empics:** Matthew Ashton *36cl*, Michael Steele *36c*; **Mary Evans Picture Library:** *9c*, Henry Grant *9cb*; **Sporting Pictures:** *35bl*, Greg Crisp *14tr*, Ali Jorge *26tc*.

Jacket: **Allsport USA:** Stephen Dunn *inside back t*; Printed courtesy of **Cincinnati Reds:** Greg Rust *front tl*, *back br*.